The Helpful Beaver

by
Sascha Nieland Allard

George Ronald
Oxford

George Ronald, Publisher
Oxford
www.grbooks.com

2025 by Sascha Nieland Allard

All Rights Reserved

A catalogue record for this book is available
from the British Library

ISBN: 978-0-85398-674-4

Illustrated by Dilmi Amarasinghe

Dedicated to all the children of the world

The Helpful Beaver

When we love one another,
there is always time to spare.
Offering help when it's needed
shows how much we care.

In a large, swampy pond lived a colony of beavers. They always worked hard and were high achievers.

These beavers were busy making their lodges strong, so they'd have cosy homes to gather in, all winter long.

They had to work quickly, and sometimes at night, for winter was coming. Their schedule was tight.

Close by was an otter
diving into the lake.
He was snapping up fish
with each splash he'd make.

Suddenly, Otter yelped –
"Please help me, I'm stuck!
My tail's got caught,
what horrible luck!"

"I wish I could help you" one beaver remarked, "but I have to collect bark before it gets dark!"

Another beaver said, "I'm busy chewing trees to get wood for my lodge. Ask someone else, please!"

A third beaver gathered sticks and mud for the floor. The lodge was its focus. Nothing else, nothing more.

Finally, there was Becky, who paused to think of how she could lend a caring paw to help Otter now.

Becky was the busiest of all,
building both a lodge and a dam.
But she knew helping was important,
so towards Otter she swam.

She dove under the water
and quickly moved the rock,
then safely lay Otter down
on the nearest wooden dock.

Becky said, "There's always time to help someone in need." Then she smiled and continued to build her lodge with speed.

Otter said, "thank you", and returned to his den.

With mud in his grip
and sticks of great size,

he came back to help Becky – what a joyful surprise!

Otter said, "These are from my den – you can use them to build."
"Oh, thank you so much!" Becky said, feeling thrilled.

Together, they quickly finished and even had time to play. They floated on their backs, enjoying the warm summer rays.

All the other beavers had work left to do,

so Becky and Otter thought,
Let's help them out too!

With Becky and Otter's help the work sped along,

With teamwork and effort, their lodges were done.

They were solid and secure for the winter to come.

They all came to see
there's always time to spare,
to help a friend in need
and show how much we care.

Discussion questions

1. How would you feel if someone helped you when you needed it?

2. How can you help someone who is feeling sick, tired or lonely?

3. What is one thing you could do today to help someone at school or at home?

4. Why is it important to help others, even if we're busy?

5. What are some ways we can be helpful to our family members?

6. What do you think would happen if no one helped anyone?

Collect them all

 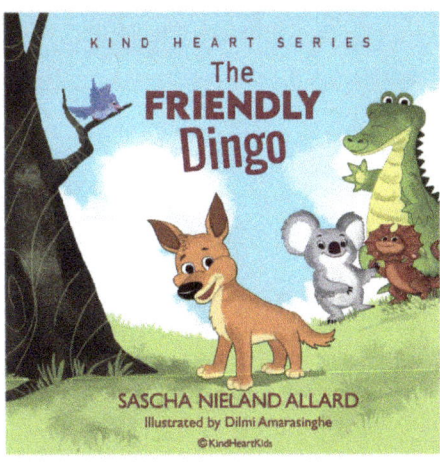 

 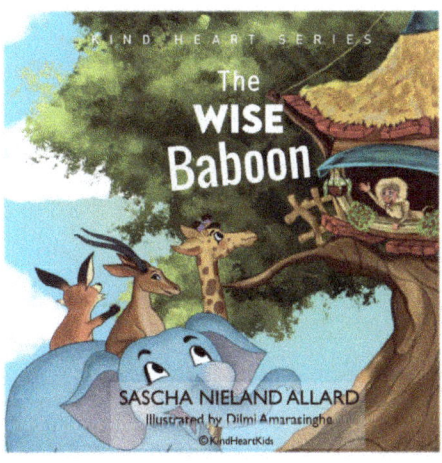 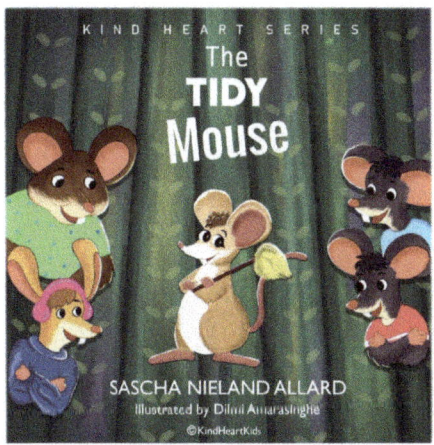

www.kindheartkids.ca
Instagram@Kindheart.kids

www.ingramcontent.com/pod-product-compliance
Lightning Source LLC
LaVergne TN
LVHW070949070426
835507LV00029B/3462